HOCKEY

Published by
The Hamlyn Publishing Group Limited
London / New York / Sydney / Toronto
Hamlyn House, Feltham, Middlesex,
England

This edition published in the
United States by
Rand McNally & Company
Chicago / New York / San Francisco

text by Trent Frayne
introduction by
Johnny Bower

Rand McNally
& Company
Chicago/New York
San Francisco

CONTENTS

Hockey is the greatest sport I know. I have been playing it as a pro since 1945, and it still holds as much excitement for me as it did when I first started out as a youngster. Every time I step on the ice I get that same tight feeling in the stomach as when I made my debut in the big-time nearly a quarter of a century ago; after every game there is still the same triumph in victory or agony in defeat. Hockey has so much to offer that it is very hard to give up—and this in spite of what a goalie has to face in the way of sustained assault on his body.

I owe hockey a great deal. It has given me and my family everything we ever wanted from life. It has provided me with a lifetime of wonderful memories of the master craftsmen of the game who have either played with or against me. It has made me as many friends as it has given me bruises.

In this book you will find all the thrills of the game as it is today. Trent Frayne has vividly described the background scene, and in Harold Barkley's photographs you will find all the action you need. I am sure their work will give hockey fans everywhere a lot of pleasure.

John Bower

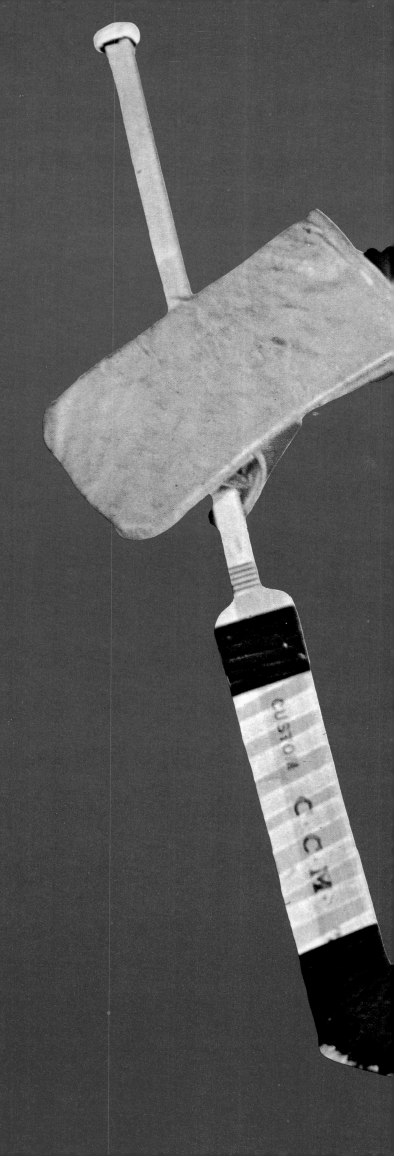

HOCKEY TODAY

In 1969 the question most often asked of a tall slender girl named Heidi Stanfield, a guide on the 55th-floor Observation Tower of the tallest building in the British Commonwealth, concerned the location of a hockey rink in midtown Toronto called Maple Leaf Gardens.

Heidi is a very beautiful girl, and Toronto has a number of historic sites, so it is a graphic measure of the hold hockey has on the Canadian public that people were more concerned with this modest segment of the national game than they were with, say, her plans for the evening or a view of any other landmark.

Hockey transcends just about everything in Canada, where Maple Leaf Gardens in Toronto and the Forum in Montreal are the focal points of the game's coast-to-coast interest. These rinks are home for the Toronto Maple Leafs and the Montreal Canadiens, the two most successful teams by far during the decade and a half since photographer Harold Barkley began shooting the colour action in this book.

In fact, with the single exception of 1961, no team other than the Canadiens or the Maple Leafs was able to win the Stanley Cup, which is emblematic of the world's professional hockey championship. And Montreal and Toronto are uninterrupted winners at the box-office. There has not been an unsold seat in either rink for professional hockey since the end of the Second World War, and both buildings have been overhauled repeatedly to provide additional seating. Each can now accommodate more than 16,000 people comfortably seated, and for this privilege patrons pay up to $6.50 each. More than ninety per cent of the seats are sold on a seasonal basis. Seats are so precious that subscribers' rights to them have even been left in wills.

Partly, of course, this is due to the fact that there is an inborn interest in hockey right across the country. It is by far the most popular of all the sports, at least in part because it is the most accessible. The moment a stream freezes over in late fall it is a glistening invitation to youngsters to skate. Most little boys in Canada are excellent skaters by the time they reach school age. Professional hockey, being an extension of this early exposure, has tens of thousands of knowledgeable followers whose interest in the game is whetted by the vast attention it gets from television, radio, magazines and newspapers.

The Gardens was opened in 1931, and even thirty-eight years later its attraction is still enormous, like that of an enduring old actor at whom people like to stare either because of what he represents or from familiarity or, perhaps, even nostalgia. 'When people get here and start looking around,' Heidi Stanfield related in the towering Toronto-Dominion Centre, 'the first question invariably is, ''Which building is Maple Leaf Gardens?''' 'Is the question mostly from little boys?' she was asked. 'From little boys,' Heidi smiled, 'of all ages.'

Interest in the Gardens and professional hockey, which are synonymous, attained a continuing coast-to-coast scope in November of 1931 with the inception of national radio broadcasts of Saturday night games in the Gardens by a young unpretentious man named Foster Hewitt whose work gave the game a dimension it had never known. Hewitt was so good, so captivating in his descriptions of play, that he attracted hundreds of thousands of people whose initial interest in hockey itself was, at best, cursory. His weekly broadcast became the most popular radio programme in Canada, and his unique style turned Saturday night hockey into an institution from the Atlantic to the Pacific all through the 1930s, the 1940s, and even into the television takeover of the 1950s when Hewitt's radio broadcasts were carried as audio on telecasts as well. Hewitt made national heroes of the sweaty serfs toiling beneath his broadcast booth, and he turned his standard phrase, 'He shoots!... He scores!' into household words.

It is doubtful if more than a small fraction of one per cent of the five million listeners his radio broadcasts attracted in Canada would have recognized Hewitt if they had engaged him in conversation. His speaking voice was restrained and soft, nothing like his sound on the air. The flamboyant voice with the trenchant tones of an evangelist that the millions of listeners knew so well belonged to an almost embarrassingly modest, retiring and colourless paradox. Even late in the 1960s, when he had long since turned his play-by-play chores over to his son Bill, Foster Hewitt was still identified with the game and the broadcasts. He spent his hockey nights selecting the outstanding three players for the network telecasts, and appearing self-consciously on camera at the end of each game to provide reasons for his selections.

So Hewitt, more than anyone else, was responsible for the fact that people all across Canada sought out a bird's-eye

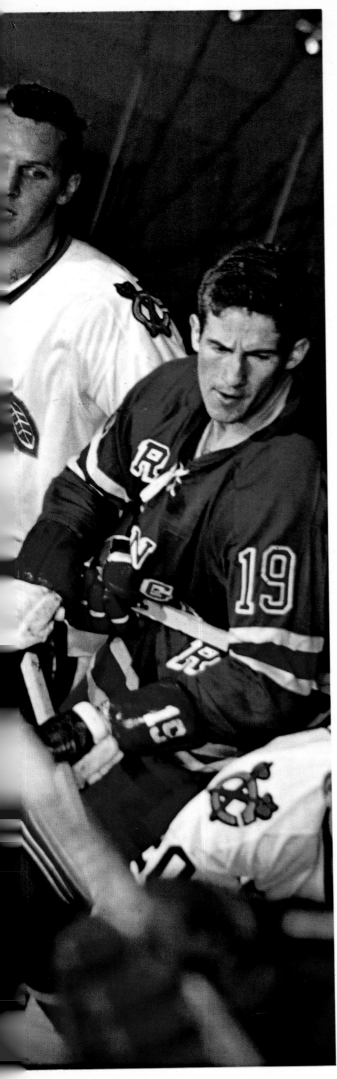

view of Maple Leaf Gardens whenever they visited the heights of the Toronto-Dominion Tower, almost forty years after he first broadcast hockey from the building he turned into a kind of shrine.

There *was* hockey before Hewitt, at least a century of it. Historians are vague on the game's precise origin, although the Canadian Amateur Hockey Association once appointed a committee to determine when it began, and one paragraph in their conclusion records: 'The first hockey was played by Royal Canadian Rifles, an Imperial unit, stationed at Halifax and Kingston in 1855. It is quite possible that English troops stationed in Kingston from 1783 to 1855 played hockey, as there is evidence in old papers, letters and legends that the men and officers located with the Imperial troops were proficient skaters and participated in field hockey. The playing of hockey games in Kingston as early as 1855 is certain.'

So the game likely began in the mid-nineteenth century when soldiers tied skates to their boots, borrowed field-hockey sticks and began crashing into one another. When forwards lifted the puck instead of skimming it along the ice in shooting it, the men in goal borrowed wicket-keepers' leg guards from cricket to protect their assaulted shins.

Modern purists point to a debilitating American influence on the game, the concessions to the US bloodlust in the loose interpretation of rules that condone fights and rough play. The charge does not survive scrutiny, however; games were as tough and blood flowed even more freely in the years preceding the game's invasion of the large US centres in the 1920s. The late Jack Adams, coach and general manager of the Detroit Red Wings for more than thirty years, once recalled a game in the pre-American era between the Toronto Arenas, for whom he played, and the Montreal Wanderers, who carved him up so freely that he came out looking like the loser of a sabre duel at Stuttgart. When the game ended he was wheeled to the Montreal General Hospital where his sister was a nurse, and, indeed, it was she who admitted him. Adams was so battered and bloodied, however, that she did not recognize him until he registered at the admitting desk. 'It wasn't an unusually tough game,' Adams said airily, years later. 'When you got cut in those days (the early 1920s) you skated to the boards where the trainer sloshed off the blood with a sponge he kept in a bucket and patched you up with a slice of adhesive tape. That night, most of my tape must have sweated off.'

The National Hockey League came into being at a meeting in the Windsor Hotel in Montreal on the night of November 22, 1917, and the first games among the four charter members were played on December 19. The Toronto Arenas were beaten 10–9 by the Montreal Wanderers in one of the two inaugural games, and the Montreal Canadiens beat the Ottawa Senators 7–4 in the other.

The rudimentary nature of the league's beginning is exemplified by this copy of a set of rules posted in the Toronto dressing quarters by the Arenas' manager, the late Charlie Querrie:

1. First and foremost do not forget that I am running this club.
2. You are being paid to give your best services to the club. Condition depends a lot on how you behave off the ice.
3. It does not require bravery to hit another man over the head with a stick. If you want to fight, go over to France. (The First World War was in its fourth year.)
4. Do not think you are putting over something on the manager when you do anything you should not. You are being paid to play hockey, not to be a good fellow.
5. I am an easy boss if you do your share. If you do not want to be on the square and play hockey, turn in your uniform and go at some other work.

The teams planned a twenty-two-game schedule in their first season but when the Westmount Arena, the home of Montreal's Wanderers, burned down, the team dropped out of the league, and the three others continued on an eighteen-game schedule.

Boston was the first American representative, joining the NHL in 1924. Pittsburgh and the New York Americans came along a year later, and in 1926 three more US teams were added – Chicago, Detroit and the Rangers in New York. By then there were ten teams divided into two divisions in this manner:

Canadian Division

Ottawa Senators
Montreal Canadiens
New York Americans
Montreal Maroons
Toronto Maple Leafs

American Division

New York Rangers
Boston Bruins
Chicago Black Hawks
Pittsburgh Pirates
Detroit Cougars

The Toronto Arenas had changed their name to the St Patricks in 1919, and they became the Maple Leafs in 1926. Detroit changed from Cougars to Falcons in 1930, and then to Red Wings in 1933. The Pittsburgh franchise was switched to Philadelphia in 1930 where it stayed for one year (the team was called the Quakers, won four games in a forty-four-game schedule, and, not surprisingly with a record like that, folded). Ottawa, once one of the great NHL cities, grew so lethargic in its support of the Senators that the team suspended operations for one year in 1931, resumed for two years, and then switched to St Louis in the fall of 1934 where it operated as the Eagles for one season and was then disbanded.

When the Montreal Maroons collapsed in 1938, the NHL was returned to a one-division set-up with seven teams, which it remained until the autumn of 1942 when the New York Americans surrendered. That left the NHL as a six-team league, and it stayed that way for the next quarter-century. Then, in the summer of 1967, expansion came again, this time in the form of six new American teams, all lumped together as the Western Division and playing inter-divisional games with the old league, now called the Eastern Division. The number of games was increased from seventy per season, which it had been since 1949, to seventy-four, and it was increased again in 1968 when the present seventy-six game grind was manfully embraced by the owners and bravely undertaken by the serfs.

Expansion took the NHL about as far west as it could go, clear out to the sooty environs of Los Angeles where a garrulous ex-Canadian named Jack Kent Cooke built a gorgeous, columned reincarnation of Rome's Colosseum and called it the Forum, and to the fog-bound reaches of San Francisco, where a youth named Barry von Gerbig settled into the ancient Cow Palace and then suddenly shifted his franchise across the bay to Oakland.

The old rink in St Louis was refurbished grandly to accommodate the St Louis Blues, a new edifice in Philadelphia housed the Flyers, a community stadium precisely half-way between Minneapolis and St Paul served as home to the Minnesota North Stars, and Pittsburgh acquired an NHL franchise for the first time since 1930 when the old Pittsburgh Pirates had sagged irretrievably after five seasons.

By the time expansion arrived, the players had banded together to form a union. In common with management everywhere, NHL front offices had for years resisted occasional timid forays

from the servants' quarters. In 1957 a majority of big-league players was brought into concord by a New York attorney, Milton N. Mound, but it was an uneasy alliance quickly dissipated by the kindly old owners.

But in the spring and summer of 1967 a Toronto lawyer, thirty-four-year-old Alan Eagleson, with solid backing from key players, undertook to organize the National Hockey League Players' Association. By midsummer he had them so thoroughly organized – 114 out of 120 of the established teams had signed pledges to him and the other half-dozen were verbally committed – that within fifteen minutes during a meeting with the owners he had them agreeing to recognize the union in a capitulation that made hockey history. He earlier had won his way into the hearts of all hockey players by extracting unprecedented amounts of money from the Boston Bruins in return for the signature of eighteen-year-old Bobby Orr, an inordinately gifted young junior player.

Boston offered Orr a $5,000 bonus to sign a two-year contract at $7,500 for the first season and $8,000 for the second. Orr's father sought out Eagleson, who readily recognized that the management of recent dreadful Boston teams was in no position to haggle over this sensational junior. He negotiated an $85,000 two-year contract for Orr – more than four times the original Boston offer. And when that contract expired, the twenty-year-old Orr was manœuvred so adroitly by Eagleson (or perhaps it was the Boston management that was adroitly manœuvred), that Orr's salary was raised to the superstar level of $90,000 a year, which turned out to be precisely one hundred times more than the $900 Jack Adams received for a full season with the Toronto Arenas in the early 1920s.

Indeed, if one were a hockey player, salaries took on delicious proportions with the coming of the Union and with Eagleson driving the bargains, or with his ominous shadow lurking over the owners' shoulders. A handsome lad from Canada's national team, Danny O'Shea, received $20,000 as a bonus for signing a professional contract with the Minnesota North Stars, plus a two-year contract at $20,000 a year. Normie Ullman of Toronto, who had recently been traded to the Maple Leafs by Detroit, got $48,000 from the Leafs in 1969, and this sum was upped to $52,000 when it was pointed out to management that Ullman had received American funds during his tenure at Detroit, so that his raise in equivalent

Canadian funds deserved to be $4,000 higher. Goalkeeper Glenn Hall staggered along on $48,000 a year at St Louis, unobtrusive Ray Cullen at just under $25,000 at Minnesota, Stan Mikita at $45,000 at Chicago, Jim Pappin at $95,000 for three years at Chicago, and Frank Mahovlich $40,000 at Detroit.

With endorsements and other outside interests considered, the two highest paid hockey players in the world are Bobby Hull and Gordie Howe. Hull, the Golden Jet of Chicago, collects $100,000 from the Black Hawks and as much again from a myriad of sources so complex as to keep a coterie of seventeen advisers and public-relations consultants involved in his affairs.

For his part, Howe has not been taking his meals at a Salvation Army hostel lately, either, although for a man who had spent twenty-two years in the biggest league in hockey he was rather late at the trough. He noted in the spring of 1969 that he would have done a great deal better in his acquisition of the world's goods if a man like lawyer Eagleson had happened along even a decade ago, but, even so, Howe has been making up for it recently. It is estimated that he takes down $70,000 a year at Detroit, he has permitted the T. Eaton Company exclusive use of his name in various merchandising projects, he travels extensively as a front man for that company in the off season, and he is involved in various enterprises in Detroit, where he has made his permanent home for fifteen years. Unlike Hull, one of whose coterie has said publicly that his boy will be close to the millionaire identity if things keep going at their present clip for another half-dozen years, Howe handles his own enterprises without benefit of seventeen advisers, and sort of ambles along quietly and unobtrusively, piling up the bucks the way he piles up goals. Endlessly.

Of the hockey heroes portrayed by Barkley in this book, five can be said to have achieved the superstar status – Hull, Howe, Orr and a pair from the Montreal Canadiens, Jean Béliveau and Maurice Richard. Curiously, they have nothing in common, at least superficially. They are all shapes and sizes, from the blocky heavy-set Hull to the rangy almost lanky Béliveau, with Howe somewhere between the two, being heavily muscled like Hull, and long-armed like Béliveau. In stature, Orr and Richard are most alike, each an inch or so under six feet and leanly compact.

What each of the five has in common, of course – or had, in the case of Richard, who retired suddenly on the eve of what would have been his nineteenth season in the NHL, in September 1960 – is an unswerving dedication to his game, an ability to shake off crippling injury, and a resolute combativeness. The miracle of Orr, of course, was that he was able to join such exalted company in so brief a tenure – the 1968–9 season was only his third in the NHL, and he did not turn twenty-one until March 20, 1969. Still, by then there was scarcely anyone to argue that he was not the finest defenceman of all time.

Orr's forte, like that of Howe, is that he can do all things required of a hockey player, and can do all of them surpassingly well. He resembles Howe, too, in the fact that his work is not spectacular. If you were to see him once, or Howe once, the chances are you would wonder what all the shouting was about. In each case, it is simply that the sum of all the parts is overwhelming.

Contrarily, it would be difficult to miss Rocket Richard and Bobby Hull even if you were to spend only five minutes in the arena. Hull is smooth and swift and his strides exude power. In recent years he has acquired a way of pacing himself that can be disarming, because he has learned his game so well that it is only when his senses tell him he has an opening that he shifts into overdrive. If an opposing player has the angle on him so that he is cut off from advancing with the puck, he will nonchalantly pass it off to another player and continue his amiable pace down the ice. But then, when the opening shows, he leaps electrifyingly into it, bulling and slanting, and, with the arms and shoulders of a paranoiac weight-lifter, rams a devastating shot at the poor goalkeeper.

For Richard's part, the man they called the Rocket scored goals from all angles and positions and often while he was carrying desperate defencemen on his back. Sometimes he scored them while lying flat on his back, with at least one defender clutching his stick, another hacking at his ankles and another grabbing his sweater. He had a remarkable sense of his position in relation to the goal, too, an unerring sense of direction that enabled him to whirl a full 180 degrees when he stood in front of the net with his back to the goalkeeper, and uncannily drill the puck into an opening without so much as a glance at the goal before he whirled and fired.

But Richard never seemed to revel in the destruction he wrought. A dark and brooding man with piercing black eyes and a pinched mouth, his features seldom departed from their melancholy cast even when he scored, and then only briefly. He would skate in tiny circles, impatiently waiting for the referee to drop the puck again after he had put it into the net. He scored 544 goals in his eighteen seasons and it is doubtful if he greeted even one of them with more than a momentary pause for joy. He just seemed to go on seething.

Richard's successor as hero in the Montreal Forum, Béliveau, is his temperamental antithesis – cool, remote, solemn, with the proud and regal bearing of a young de Gaulle. He is an arresting figure of six-feet-three and weighs some 205 pounds, with handsome, sharply defined features, and a warm infrequent smile. What he appears to bring most to the Canadiens is stability, a kind of glacial quality of leadership.

It was mentioned earlier that the five superstars shared in common an unswerving dedication to hockey. There is another common factor, which may or may not be significant: all of them emerged from big, hard-working families that raised big, self-reliant kids, families that lived and grew up by the sweat of their brows and earned their own earthy kind of distinction, starting from scratch in the face of hardship and competition.

Gordie Howe was born fifth in a family of nine on the wheat-growing prairies of Saskatchewan at a little place called Floral. That was on March 31, 1928. Béliveau, born August 31, 1931, in Three Rivers, Quebec, was the first-born of five sons and three daughters. Rocket Richard came from a family of four boys and four girls born in Bordeaux on the outskirts of Montreal, where his father built freight cars in the CPR shops; Maurice was born there on August 4, 1921. Bobby Hull was the fifth child and first boy in a family of eleven at Pointe Anne, Ontario, four miles east of Belleville on the Bay of Quinte. And that was on January 3, 1939. Three years later, Hull's father insists, Bobby could skate. The family home was only a hundred yards from the bay and on the Christmas before Bobby turned four, his father bought skates for him and two sisters, who were seven and six. Mrs Hull sent the three kids to the bay with their skates and the admonition that 'the first one who comes in, the skates go back to Santa'. Hull's father swears that the lad was skating passably well within fifteen minutes, and that the only way the family could get the youngsters back for dinner was to go and get them.

One other of the eleven Hulls turned out to be a fine hockey player, Bobby's younger brother Dennis, nearly six years his junior, who joined the Chicago Black Hawks in the autumn of 1964 and came up with his most productive season during the 1968–9 campaign, though constantly overshadowed by you-know-who.

Bobby Orr's family is small, but only by comparison. The young Bruin superstar is the third of five children of Doug and Arva Orr, who live in Parry Sound, Ontario, 140 miles north of Toronto. Orr, like the other four superstars, showed an early self-reliance, and perhaps this attribute is the legacy of a large family where there is no time for one child to be coddled. For his first season at Oshawa, some 150 miles south of Parry Sound, Bobby commuted to games when his parents or friends drove the 300-mile round trip. The next year he moved to Oshawa and was on his own, a well-adjusted, thoughtful, fifteen-year-old youngster.

Hull left home even earlier – at fourteen. His mother recalls that when he first went away to play hockey he was homesick, so in her daily letters to him she rarely mentioned the family and spoke only in generalities. He told her when he got home once between games: 'Gee, Mom, keep those letters coming with nothing in them.' When he was growing up, it was a rare winter's day that Bobby was not skating and playing hockey. After heavy snowfalls he would be the first kid on the near-by bay, skating behind a wide shovel to clear snow. That, he has said since, may account for his heavy chest and arm development; that, and the fact he played all sports energetically and endlessly, and worked on neighbouring farms or a near-by cement plant in the summertime.

Hull reached the NHL at eighteen. By the time he had turned twenty-one he was the league's leading scorer, and he just went on from peak to peak, a full-blown Canadian hero who had the kids packed round him wherever hockey was played, jamming and buzzing for his autograph. One time he returned to Chicago after a long road trip anxious to see his own four boys, but there were fully 300 people awaiting his arrival at Chicago's O'Hare Airport. When Hull stepped through the arrival gate, mobs of people surged towards him. Youngsters flung all shapes of paper and cards at him for his autograph, and a dozen or so men and women popped flash cameras at him, shouting and shoving to clear paths for their pictures. Two of Bobby's own boys, whom their mother had brought to the airport, stood on either side of their father, holding on to his knees, staring up at him as he signed the endless stream of papers, two solemn little eggs impassively waiting for their dad. Hull stood there for eighteen minutes by the clock, writing his name over and over, fixing a smile as now and then a flash-bulb exploded.

Kids ringed themselves around Rocket Richard in his time, too, but the Rocket, predictably, did not have much time for autographing sessions. It was not that he disliked youngsters particularly—indeed, he sired and adored six of his own—but he was such an emotionally charged man in his hockey days that he could not abide the tedium.

Richard was making his way in hockey at seventeen, and, of course, had played the game from early childhood. His young brother, Henri, later a star in his own right with the Canadiens, was only six years old when Maurice left home so he rarely saw him. The Rocket was still with the Canadiens when Henri made the grade, but the two of them rarely exchanged conversation in the dressing-room. Maurice never gave Henri advice and Henri was so constituted that he never sought it. Maurice was terribly proud of Henri, in his own way, racing to aid him any time Henri became involved in difficulty on the ice. Once Henri had proved himself, though, aid was no longer required and, accordingly, not forthcoming.

Family friends recall that all eight of the Richard children had this reserve. Toe Blake, who was Richard's teammate for many years before Blake became the Canadien coach, once recalled a dimension of his young teammate's retiring nature. An American reporter asked Blake if the Rocket spoke English; he wanted to interview him after a game in New York.
'I'm not sure that he even speaks French,' Blake grinned kindly. 'He just doesn't speak.'

As a youngster Gordie Howe endeavoured to overcome a lack of minerals in his infancy, which had left him with a weak spine, by working for a building construction company, mixing cement, and by hanging from the archways of doors and swinging his hips for hour upon hour. As a result he has a thick upper body, with large sloping shoulders, big arms and strong wrists. Howe left home at sixteen to move to eastern Canada where he played for the Galt juniors, some fifty miles west of Toronto and a good 2,500

miles east of his home. He turned professional at seventeen and went to the corn-husking State of Nebraska to a Detroit farm club at Omaha. In a fight with defenceman Myles Lane young Howe was knocked to the ice by a savage blow. He climbed to his feet, and was knocked down again. Once more he gained his feet, ducked a wild swing by Lane, and tore into him and gave him a good lacing.

That night his coach phoned the Detroit boss, Jack Adams, told him of the courage shown by the lanky youngster (who, incidentally, had scored twenty-two goals for Omaha) and that was enough for Adams. He promoted Howe to the NHL, and Gordie became one of the most remarkable professional athletes of all time. By 1969 he had scored 700 goals (only Hull, Béliveau and Richard have scored more than 400), played his 1,500th game in the NHL, been credited with his 900th assist and his 1,600th scoring point (a combination of goals and assists), and all of these achievements represented plateaus never before even approached by any other player.

Jean Béliveau was attracting attention from the professionals by the time he was sixteen in the little town of Victoriaville in Quebec province. The coach of the Victoriaville team, one Rollie Hebert, recommended him to Frank Selke, a wise tiny man who ran the Montreal Canadiens. But the owner of a junior team in Quebec City, Frank Byrne, had heard of Béliveau even earlier. A goalkeeper named Lucien Duchene, who had played junior for Byrne, telephoned him from Victoriaville. 'Frank, you've got to come right down,' Duchene said. 'There's a kid here, maybe sixteen, who practised with our senior club today and he damn near knocked my head off with a shot. He's big and he's all bone.'

Béliveau became a great player in Quebec City, and then in 1953 he moved on to Montreal, a little later than the other four superstars in moving to the major league. He was twenty-two and had dallied in Quebec City where senior hockey was as attractive to the fans as junior. And in Béliveau's case, the money paid in this so-called amateur league was as attractive as that offered by the pros. He was collecting $20,000 a season in those far-off days, and he was a ready-made star the moment he stepped into the National Hockey League.

Once, the goalkeeper's job was the old folks' home of hockey, a peaceful, gainful retreat where men like Tiny Thompson,

Davie Kerr, Lorne Chabot and George Hainsworth played on and on and on. They collected a bruise here and a lump there, but in an era of close-checking forwards and bone-displacing defence-men, theirs was an occupation of infrequent, tranquil turnover.

Then came rule changes that turned the rinks into the shooting galleries they are now, and the goalkeeper soon became the most vulnerable man in the game, an emotional as well as a physical victim of the speed-up. In the modern fervour of near constant rush-hour traffic in the goalmouth, of screened shots and deflected shots and power plays and seventy-six-game schedules ranging from Montreal to Los Angeles and from San Francisco to New York, it is the rare bird who holds up even for a single season without a vacation to rest an aching back, a gaping cut, or a tortured mind.

All goalies undergo a kind of tension that is unique to their profession. The very nature of their work prevents them from giving free rein to their emotions. Defencemen can rid themselves of tension by knocking down an opposing forward, and forwards can tear up and down in pursuit of the puck, offsetting mental pressure with physical impact. Goal-keepers just stand there.
'They look impassive but they boil inside,' Murray (Muzz) Patrick once noted. Patrick, son of one of the pro game's builders, the late Lester Patrick, coached the New York Rangers for a couple of seasons in the mid-1950s before becoming a front-office executive. 'The truth is, they play a different game,' he expanded. 'The closest approach in another sport might be the catcher in baseball. But still, he does things that *are* baseball – goes up to hit, chases foul flies and so on. But the goalie does nothing that the other hockey players do. Except for his sweater, the guy even dresses differently.'

Through most of the 1960s one of the more remarkable men in hockey was Toronto goalkeeper Johnny Bower, who reached the NHL in 1958 after a dozen years in the minors at Vancouver, Cleveland and Providence.

After that, in the latter stages of his decade and more with the Maple Leafs, Bower became as celebrated for the fact of his age as of his ability, and he was heavily endowed with both.

No one, including Bower, was quite sure of his age, since his birth certificate was lost in his early youth. In the late 1960s whenever he had to sign a document requiring his age, he would put down any figure that happened to pop into his head—forty-three sometimes, forty-six other times, forty-four if the spirit moved him.

The *NHL Guide*, hockey's more-or-less official record book, recorded his birth date as November 8, 1924, and that was as good a reflection of his true age as any. Accordingly, he was leaping around his goal in the most acrobatic of styles in his early forties, earning the Vezina Trophy in 1965 when he was probably forty-one. Two years later he helped the Leafs win the Stanley Cup, combining with Terry Sawchuk in a truly astonishing display to eliminate Chicago and then Montreal in the playoffs.

Of him, his coach Punch Imlach once said: 'John Bower is the most remarkable athlete in professional sports. Show me any man of his age who fills a job half as tough as keeping goal in this league. I don't think there is one.'

The injuries incurred by goalies, and their equanimity in the face of them, jar the senses. Terry Sawchuk has had 400 stitches, literally, taken in his face and head alone, and incredibly these are the least of his problems. On his eighteenth birthday his eyeball was cut by a skate, and only an emergency operation saved his sight in the injured eye. Doctors reported he was on the verge of a nervous breakdown when he quit hockey half-way through the 1957 season (he was back in '58). In 1954 he was in an automobile accident and suffered a collapsed lung, but this did not interfere with his hockey career, either. He suffered a spinal condition called lordosis for years which caused such severe pain that he could not sleep for more than two hours at a stretch. In the spring of 1966 his left side became numb and he was fearful that he had suffered a stroke. But medical examination established that he had two herniated discs in his back. It was thought if the operation were successful his hockey career would be over, but Sawchuk accepted the risk and continued to play.

Sawchuk, a tall, big-boned man who will be forty in December 1969, once went to the Detroit training camp weighing 229 pounds. He was admittedly overweight, but a few years later, in the playoffs for Toronto, he stepped on the scales after a tough game, haggard, drawn, his body a mass of blue and yellow and purple welts, and the needle on the weighing machine stopped at 157, exactly seventy-two pounds less than his weight that autumn in Detroit.

As remarkable a man, though a considerably less injured one, is Glenn Hall,

who hates his job but plays it because he can find no other way to make a good living. Hall joined the St Louis Blues, one of the expansion teams, after a historic career with Detroit and Chicago during one stretch of which he played 552 consecutive games without any form of relief from duty, a record that will stand for ever. (Nowadays, a goalkeeper who plays 552 consecutive *minutes* feels he is earning his keep.)
'I sometimes ask myself what the hell I am doing out here,' Hall related once. 'But it's the only way I can support my family. If I could do it some other way I wouldn't be playing goal.'

Sportswriter Jim Hunt, pointing out that the once amiable and pleasant Hall had been turned into a gloomy lone-wolf by the torment of his job, asked the goalkeeper if he would like to take a front-office job in preference to facing incoming forwards.
'That would be worse than playing,' Hall said. 'I'd have to put up with sportswriters and fans, and I'd have to think of pleasant things to say. I couldn't stand that.'

Even after fourteen seasons and at the age of thirty-eight, Hall suffers from such tension before a hockey game that he is ill to his stomach before he takes the ice. He has found that hot tea laced with sugar calms his stomach better than any other remedy, and he sips this before games and during intermissions.

In the autumn of 1968 Hall was joined in St Louis by another remarkable practitioner, Jacques Plante. Plante was making a comeback at thirty-nine (he turned forty before the season was half over) after ten years with the Montreal Canadiens and two more with the New York Rangers, and then retiring in the spring of 1965 after one season in the minors at Baltimore.

The Canadiens rid themselves of Plante in spite of the fact he had won the Vezina Trophy as the league's top goaltender in six of his ten years with them. The charge was hypochondria which the Canadiens seemed to feel bordered on the maniacal. Plante felt he had asthma, but the Canadiens seemed to become aware of it only on the day of a game. 'How can a man be all right on Friday evening and show up sick on Saturday?' the team's manager, Frank Selke, once asked plaintively.

Plante lived in a different hotel from his teammates during visits to Toronto, on the grounds that the team hotel had something in the air that assaulted his sensitive breathing apparatus. Once he complained of a bad knee, but X-rays

found no damage and management accused him again of malingering.

Stubborn Jacques had a knee operation, explaining 'they opened my knee, not my head'. When three pieces of cartilage were removed from his knee, Jacques was exultant.

He liked to knit. He used to knit himself woollen caps, or tuques, in radiant colours, but the coach frowned on headgear and ordered Jacques to cease and desist. So Jacques knit undershirts for himself, and announced they felt 'very nice, quite warm, you know?'

Jacques was a man of many talents. He opened a beauty parlour in Montreal, and sometimes set hair himself.

But for all of his unusual traits, Plante revolutionized two aspects of goalkeeping. He invented a mask and he turned peripatetic. A favourite ploy of attacking teams used to be to fire the puck around the curved boards at the end of the rink so that a teammate could pick up the puck at the opposite side of the rink where often he would be standing uncovered. Plante put an end to that by whirling artfully out of his net as the puck was fired, and intercepting it before it zipped behind the goal to a waiting attacker. This move not only scuttled the attack, it gave Plante's team possession of the puck.

The manœuvre helped in a small way; the introduction of the face-mask was a major contribution. Some old-guard goalkeepers refused to follow Plante's lead, but others did—Terry Sawchuk insisted the mask had added years to his career—and more and more young goalkeepers are coming into the league wearing masks, which means that facial injuries are being increasingly reduced in this trying trade.

Plante first wore his mask on the night of November 2, 1959, and he got permission from his coach, Toe Blake, the hard way. He had been experimenting with facial protection in practice but hard-nosed Blake refused to let him wear it in games, probably on the grounds that someone would think his goalkeeper lacked courage. Far better that he break his nose or take multiple stitches in his face than *that*.

At any rate, on the night in question, Andy Bathgate of the New York Rangers rifled a puck at the Montreal net which Plante stopped beautifully with his nose. Bleeding profusely, he was led to the infirmary where seven stitches were taken in his swelling bugle. This was the era before hockey teams carried spare goalkeepers, so it was necessary to delay

the game while Plante was hem-stitched. And because of the wound, and the resultant swelling, the coach did not object when Plante reached resolutely into his locker and brought out his mask. The Canadiens won, and he wore it ever after.

Actually, it was ridiculous what Plante endured before getting his face covered. He had been experimenting with a mask for five years in practice, endeavouring to perfect one that would eliminate all visual problems. Maskless in games during that period he was cut for some 200 stitches in his face, had his nose broken four times, both cheekbones broken, and his skull fractured.

Goalkeepers ought to be allowed their idiosyncrasies; their responsibilities are out of all proportion to those of the people around them. Forwards, defence-men, the coach, even the smiling old owners can be allowed an allotment of errors, but it is a rare goalkeeping mistake that does not cost the team dearly. Obviously, unless fate intervenes in the form of a goalpost, each mistake by a goalie results in a goal. Coaches expect the padded punching-bags in the nets to make occasional mistakes, of course, but they cannot abide too many. Indeed, the way coaches assess goalkeepers in ability is not by how often they are brilliant, but by how seldom they are bad.

'A great goalie will play a poor game only five per cent of the time,' Toronto coach George 'Punch' Imlach has said. 'A good one will let you down maybe ten per cent of his games, and you just can't bother keeping one around who will be ineffective twenty-five per cent of the time.'

There is an added responsibility for the man who plays goal for a team high in the league standings. The league has a bonus system presumably designed to make teams try harder all year long. Each player on the team that ends the regular season in first place collects $2,250. The second-place team gets $1,250 per player, third-place $750, and the fourth team $250. There are similar rewards for advance-ment in the playoffs. Thus, when the Montreal Canadiens finished on top of the Eastern Division standings in the spring of 1968, won the division's playoff cham-pionship, and then beat the Western Division champions, the St Louis Blues, in the Stanley Cup final, bonus awards accruing to each Canadiens player reached $9,750.

So the impact of a goalkeeper's mis-takes becomes apparent. For example, if the Canadiens had been eliminated from the first round of the playoffs after finish-ing the season on top of their division, each player's bonus would have been reduced to $3,750, a loss of exactly $6,000.

What this responsibility can do to a man was graphically illustrated in the mid-1960s by Lorne (Gump) Worsley, a carefree popular gnome in the net of the New York Rangers for a decade. Worsley gradually developed into a troubled worrywart after he was traded to the Canadiens in 1963. In New York his life may have been at stake but there was small pressure. The Rangers played badly most of his decade there, from 1952 to 1963, but he was light-hearted and free of nagging responsibility. Indeed, one week-end after Montreal and Chicago forwards had bombarded the Rangers into two big losses, Gump was asked which team gave him the most trouble. 'The Rangers,' said Worsley without a moment's hesitation.

Since the Rangers were so palpably inept there was no pressure on any par-ticular one of them, but the atmosphere was changed drastically for blithe-spirit Worsley when he went to Montreal. There, Forum fans regard their team as slumping if the game ends in a tie.

Worsley began developing curious and inexplicable ailments, like a nervous stomach and sleeplessness and even a fear of flying. What most of his turmoil boiled down to, of course, was a reaction to his new involvement with tension, press-ure and responsibility.

Yet the Worsleys and the Plantes, the Halls, the Bowers and the Sawchuks keep responding valorously when the lights dim in the arenas at the start of games and the band (or the organ or the amplified tapes) plays the national anthem. This is the moment when the men of iron are separated from those of softer stuff.

There are really two seasons each year in the National Hockey League. There is the one that starts early each October and endures through seventy-six games for each team until the end of March. Then there is the one that takes up early in April, called the Stanley Cup playoffs, a seemingly endless elimination affair which eventually declares a champion about the middle of May.

The purpose of the seventy-six-game schedule, apart from placing vast sums of money in the owners' vaults, is to qualify eight of the twelve NHL teams for the Stanley Cup pursuit. The system is involved, but works out like this:

After seventy-six games, the four top teams in the Eastern Division and the four top teams in the Western Division engage in elimination series in their own divisions to produce divisional champions. The top team and the third-place team in each of the divisions play a four-of-seven series, while the second-place team and the fourth-place team in each division are engaged in a similar four-of-seven series. That eliminates four teams, two from each division.

Next, the survivors in each division play semi-final rounds to eliminate two more teams, again in four-of-seven series. That leaves only two survivors of the original eight contestants, each the winner of its own division, and now these two get together for still another four-of-seven series to declare the Stanley Cup champion.

Since hockey teams open their fall training camps early each September and undertake exhibition games almost immediately, it is only through June, July and August that the owners find their cash registers silent, and hockey players find their wives. Counting pre-season exhibitions, the regular season, and the playoffs, the modern professional hockey player is involved in well over 100 games a year.

By far the most successful team, year in and year out in this awful grind, is the Montreal Canadiens, whether it is through the long winter en route to the league championship or in the spring when the seemingly interminable Stanley Cup playoffs roll round. In the two decades from the autumn of 1948 to the spring of 1969, the Canadiens never

finished worse than third in the standings, were second eight times and on top of the heap nine times. In the playoffs, they reached the Stanley Cup's final round fourteen times, won the trophy nine times, and did not miss the playoffs even once.

The Canadiens, in flashing red shirts, and stressing speed, speed, speed, have been the game's most colourful team by far, and even their Gallic names have lent a glow to hockey over the years – men like the first of the great goalkeepers, Georges Vezina, called the Chicoutimi Cucumber, a cool customer on the ice, obviously, but something of a tiger at home in the little Quebec town of Chicoutimi where he sired twenty-two children. In Vezina's time there were other Montreal giants, like Armand Mondou, Pit Lepine, Battleship Leduc, Wildor Larochelle, Aurel Joliat, Black Cat Johnny Gagnon and Billy Coutu. Later there came Maurice (The Rocket) Richard, Jean Béliveau, Jacques Plante, Jean-Guy Talbot, Bernie (Boom Boom) Geoffrion, and Henri (Pocket Rocket) Richard, and still later Rogatien Vachon, Jacques Laperriére, J.-C. Tremblay, Yvan Cournoyer and Jacques Lamaire. What a Gallic galaxy!

But perhaps shining over them all was not a dashing star of French extraction or even one of the numerous great English-Canadians who have made their mark with Les Canadiens – no, the greatest of them all perhaps was a German from Stratford, Ontario, named Howie Morenz. His German descent, the Habitant management concluded when he joined the team in the autumn of 1924, might not be good box-office in predominantly French-speaking Quebec, so he was publicized as a Swiss.

Howie Morenz was more than merely one of the greatest of hockey players. He became a part of the national folklore, a symbol of a hockey era that is now only a memory, of a time when ice heroes were a rough-hewn and usually hard-drinking bunch, fiercely loyal to their teams. Even the smoke-filled rinks in which they played had a warmer look and smell than the antiseptic palaces that came along in the years of the NHL's expansion.

To the millworkers and tram-drivers and off-duty cabbies who jammed the rush end of the Forum and called themselves, with magnificent irony, the Millionaires, Morenz was a superhuman figure. Between periods they toasted him in bathtub gin. Their battle-cry, 'Les Canadiens sont là!' never reached such frenzy as when Morenz started winding

up behind his own net with a quaint little bouncing jig that sent him hurtling down the ice in an exhilarating moment of excitement that reached its crescendo when he threw himself between the defencemen and crashed the puck past the goalkeeper.

The Flying Frenchmen, curiously, had their genesis in a conversation between a Scottish baker and an Irish contractor one December night in 1909. There was then only one professional hockey league in the country, the Eastern Canada Hockey Association, and it was not flourishing. Hoping to strengthen it, James Strachan, the manager of the Montreal Wanderers, a Montrealer whose family was prominent in the baking industry, made a thoughtful remark to young Ambrose O'Brien of Renfrew, Ontario, whose father had made a good deal of money as a railway contractor. 'A team composed entirely of French-Canadian players in Montreal, with its seventy per cent French population, is bound to be a success,' Strachan said.

O'Brien at that moment was not interested. He wanted his home-town team, the Renfrew Millionaires, to win the Stanley Cup and made application to the Eastern Canada league for its admittance. When the application was refused, he remembered Strachan's remark, and set out to form his own league. He founded and financed the Montreal Canadiens on December 10, 1909, depositing $5,000 in a St James Street bank to guarantee players' salaries. They got a series of post-dated cheques that could be stopped at the bank if any player defected. He commissioned Jack Laviolette, an itinerant hockey player and owner of a restaurant in Montreal called Jack's Café, to put together a team for the $5,000.

To round out his league, O'Brien urged James Strachan to transfer his Montreal Wanderers to it, brought in the Renfrew Millionaires, and financed two teams in the booming mining belt of northern Ontario, at Cobalt and Haileybury. He called the league the National Hockey Association, and it turned out to be the forerunner of the National Hockey League.

The move by O'Brien caused an upheaval out of which the Ottawa Senators and the Montreal Shamrocks withdrew from the Eastern Canada league and joined the NHA, bringing an end to the tottering Eastern league.

The season began on January 5, 1910 with the Canadiens playing Cobalt in a tiny noisy smoke-filled firetrap called the Jubilee Rink. They attracted just under

3,000 fans and the Canadiens were indeed comprised entirely of French-Canadian players. Soon they added English-Canadians to the line-up, and they won their first Stanley Cup in 1916. The following year the NHL was formed, and the Canadiens were one of the original four teams.

In the spring of 1919 the Canadiens were involved in the only Stanley Cup final ever suspended. They were playing the Seattle Metropolitans in that West-coast city in the State of Washington during an influenza epidemic. All but three players caught the 'flu. Joe Hall, a great centre, refused to take to his bed and wore his Canadien sweater until he dropped. Two days later he died. The series was cancelled.

The club was put on the auction block in October 1921. Out of a flurry of bidding that started at $8,000, Montrealer Leo Dandurand and two partners, who owned a race-track in Cleveland, had their representative, Canadien coach Cecil Hart, buy the club for them for $11,000. It took them three years to build another Stanley Cup winner, employing the haphazard scouting methods of the era. Indeed, Dandurand, an urbane and mannered man, acquired Morenz almost by chance.

He happened to encounter a referee, Ernest Sauvé, the morning after a junior game. Sauvé advised him to look closely at this young Stratford player. The Toronto St Pat's were also interested in Morenz but the immortal Howie later admitted he signed with the Canadiens because Dandurand paid a $45 tailor's bill and gave him $300 to settle a number of small debts. His salary for the twenty-four-game schedule was $3,500, and the contract was signed on July 7, Dandurand's birthday. Accordingly, Dandurand assigned Morenz sweater number 7. Eleven years later, in the autumn of 1934 when Dandurand traded a crestfallen Morenz to Chicago, he tendered him a going-away dinner and announced that no other player would ever wear Morenz's number. None ever has.

A year later Dandurand sold the club to the Canadian Arena Company, headed by Senator Donat Raymond, for $165,000. Raymond brought back Morenz and just when it appeared he was making a strong comeback, Morenz broke a leg. He died in hospital, apparently of a heart attack, on March 8, 1937. His body was placed at centre ice in the Forum and Canadien players formed a guard of honour as 15,000 people moved slowly and silently into the rink for the service. Outside, thousands more stood with heads bared in a moving tribute to this great player.

Morenz symbolized the era of the workingman hockey player; Rocket Richard became the early symbol of the modern smartly attired young business-men off the ice, although on it they can still incite a riot. Which, indeed, they did on St Patrick's Day in 1955. Richard had been suspended for hitting a referee. Vociferously objecting fans broke up a game between the Canadiens and the Detroit Red Wings by hurling a tear-gas bomb on the Forum ice. Outside, those who could not get in on the festivities indoors did $30,000 worth of breaking and looting.

By 1957 the value of the Canadiens had increased to something more than a million dollars, the price reportedly paid by Senator Hartland Molson on behalf of the brewing company which bore his family name and of which he was President. The Molsons were still in command when expansion came to the NHL in the summer of 1967 but by that time owners had inflated notions of the value of their hockey clubs. Each of the new teams was compelled to pay $2 million for the right to join the NHL and to draft a collection of discards from the rosters of the existing teams.

Or, at any rate, it was presumed by the established teams that they were un-loading discards; as it turned out, the new teams did surprisingly well in their first season, 1967–8, and even better in their second. Indeed, by the spring of 1969 it was often difficult to differentiate between the old and the new in inter-divisional games. On one particular Sunday afternoon when the Columbia Broadcasting System was televising a game across the United States and the Canadian Television Network was carrying it in Canada, the practically incubator-fresh Minnesota North Stars humiliated the long-established Toronto Maple Leafs 7–2.

Even so, the next morning there was the usual rush to the windows overlooking Toronto in the tower of the tallest building in the Commonwealth. There, Heidi Stanfield, the beautiful guide, answered the endless question 'Which building is Maple Leaf Gardens?' with a sigh and a lacquered-fingered indication that it was that domed building right over there.

Trent Frayne

AROUND THE RINK

1/2 Toe Blake, for thirteen seasons the driving force behind the Canadiens. During this period Montreal finished first nine times and were eight times Stanley Cup champions. **1** He appears to be administering rough justice to Ralph Backstrom and Johnny Ferguson. **2** The two men who with Blake epitomize Montreal—Jean Béliveau and Maurice Richard, the Rocket.

3 The perils of goalkeeping. Gerry Desjardins in an attitude of prayer as Ron Ellis showers him with ice chips and nearly fells him with his stick.

1

2

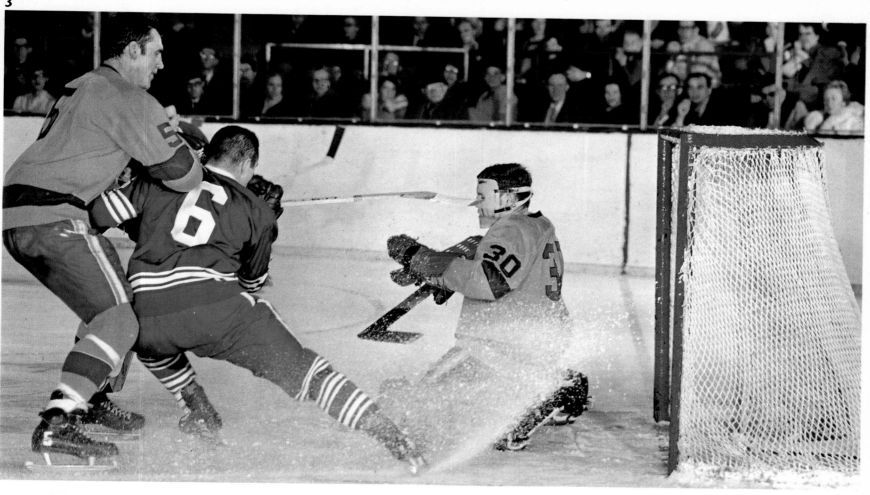

4 The Montreal player on the deck raises a leg to acknowledge Gump Worsley, thirty-nine years young and agile as ever.
5 Gary Smith, Oakland's huge goalie, saves from former Toronto teammates Floyd Smith and Norm Ullman.
6 Action concentrated in a small area. Rousseau gets his pass in before Horton's lunge can block it.

4

5

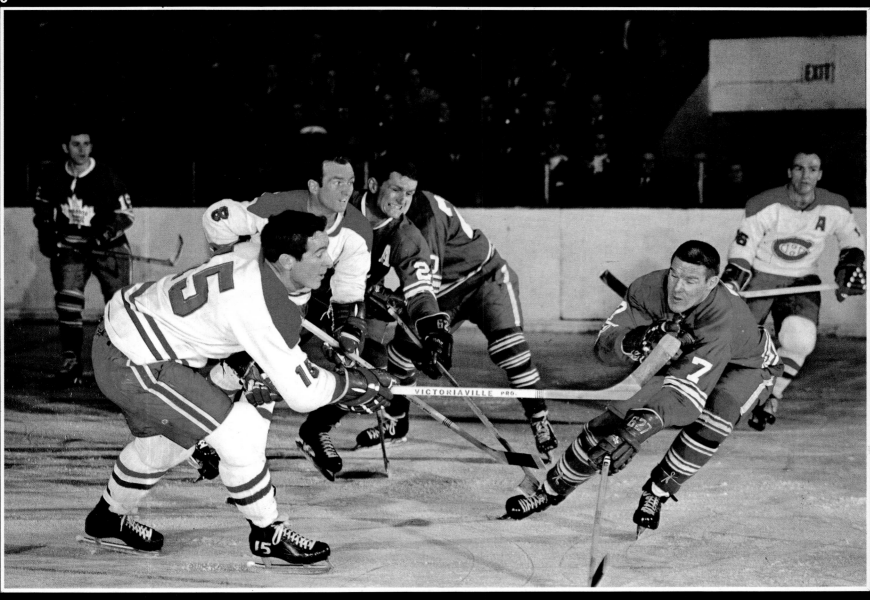

7 It takes five Black Hawks to stop the Pocket Rocket as he moves in on goal.
8 Béliveau and Tremblay seem keen that the Chicago goalie should head for the net, but the referee has other ideas.
9 Wherever the shot is coming from, Boston goalie Ed Johnston is anxious to get a sight of it.

9

10 Speed, poise and anticipation. McDonald and Mikita swivel in front of the Montreal net while Jacques Plante looks to his teammate with an expression that not even his mask can hide.

11 Fred Stanfield and Terry Harper boarding behind goal. The peanut-vendor remains noticeably unperturbed.
12/13 The dressing-room where it begins and ends. **12** Stan Mikita seems happy with his lot. The familiar features in **13** tell a different story.

14 Frustrated Red Wing takes to the air. A shot from a Detroit-Montreal game in the days when Jacques Plante (The Masked Marvel) was the most original and effective goalie in the league.

15/16 The Stanley Cup **15** in Maple Leaf hands. It was under the guidance of Punch Imlach **16** that they carried off this trophy four times between 1962 and 1967.

17 Spectators' view of play from behind the Maple Leafs' goal.

15

16

17

18 Billy Reay, coach to the Black Hawks, watches impassively but Bobby Hull, in one of his rare rest periods, is quick to voice his opinion.

19 Hockey in miniature. The pattern of play in front of goal during a Toronto-Minnesota game.

20 Aggression in defence. North Stars Wayne Hillman and Garry Bauman adopt goalmouth poses that threaten extinction to any Maple Leaf attacker.

21 Aggression in attack. Sticks poised to swing as Minnesota's Claude Larose clashes with Bruce Gamble, but the puck is still loose and the Toronto defence is mustered to clear.

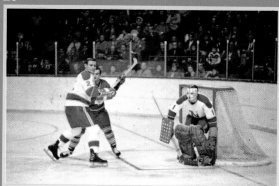

ATTACKERS

22 Gilles Marotte and Howie Young sweep out of defence in perfect formation, leaving Bob Nevin stranded on the ice.

23 The Red Wing goalie made his move too early; Bob Pulford made no mistake with his shot.
24 Ted Green is doing his best to hold Frank Mahovlich, but it needs more than a stick check to stop this great forward. Mahovlich moved to Detroit in 1968.
25 Goal! Rangers' Larry Jeffrey raises his stick in triumph while Bruins Mackenzie and Johnston can only register despair.
26 Eddie Shack being hooked by Boston's John Mackenzie as Ted Green closes in. Shack, formerly Mr Entertainer with Toronto, is now a responsible left-winger with the Bruins.

23

24

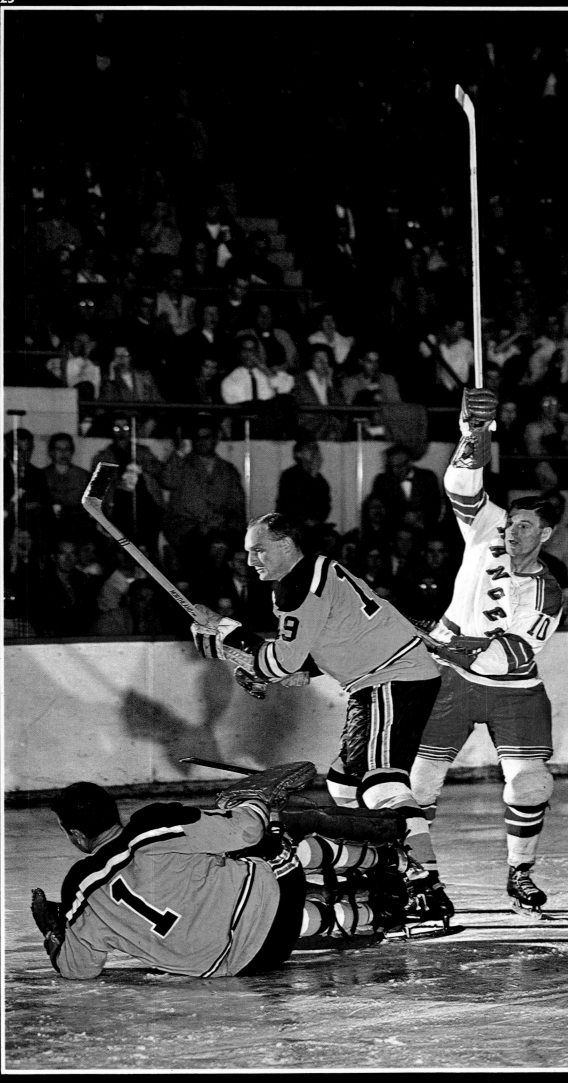

27 A dangerous moment for the Bruins with the puck loose and the goalie way out of his crease.
28 Dick Duff, Canadiens' experienced left-winger, who made a great comeback in the 1967–8 season with twenty-five goals after a lean time the year before.
29 Dave Keon, the tireless little centre, who is a fine exponent of Punch Imlach's forechecking approach to hockey.
30 Two veterans from the St Louis Blues– Al Arbour and Dickie Moore. Arbour is the only NHL player to wear spectacles on the ice.

31 Boston's Bob Perrault bellyflops painfully but manages to save from Dave Keon.
32 Bobby Hull's famous curved stick comes round to cut off Bobby Rousseau's pass.
33 A player who needs no introduction and who is never far from the action—Chicago's Stan Mikita, seen here causing disruption in the Toronto goalmouth.
34 Dennis Hull, the Golden Jet's younger brother, is not a superstar but he shares at least one thing in common with the famous Bobby—an explosive shot.

32

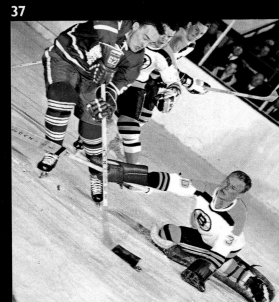

37

35 Johnny Bower has his goal well covered but Chicago's Chico Maki is in possession.
36 Red Kelly, twenty seasons a top NHL player and now coach to the Los Angeles Kings, seen here in action during his days as a centreman with the Maple Leafs.
37 Gerry Cheevers is out of his crease and looks to have no chance of preventing Frank Mahovlich from scoring.

DEFENDERS

38 Carol Vadnais, the Seals' French-Canadian defenceman, has time to assess the danger in the shape of Dave Keon before clearing.

39 The formidable Detroit defence combination of Bobby Baun and Kent Douglas, here frustrating George Armstrong. Douglas uses the heaviest stick in the game, a thirty-ounce model that is almost twice as weighty as normal. Baun relies on his own poundage.

40 Bobby Orr, the Bruins all-star, proves that he is not just the most proficient defenceman in the league; he can also fire in a lethal shot.

38

39

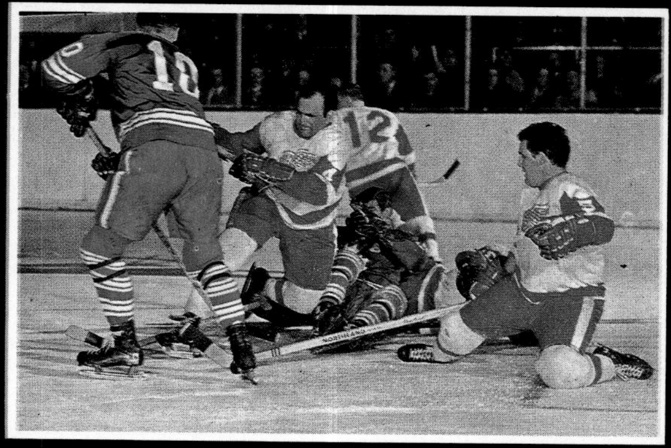

40

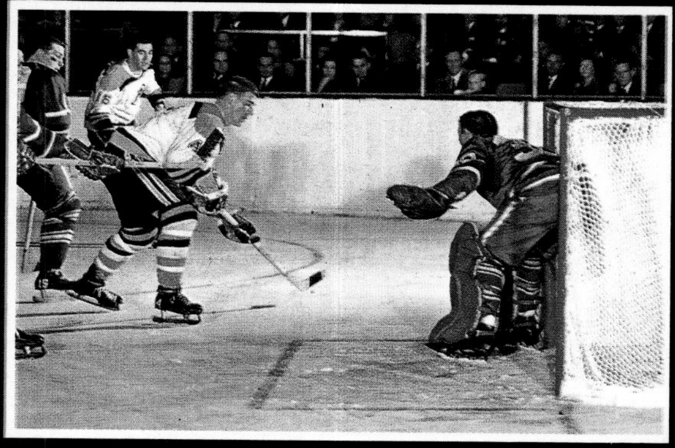

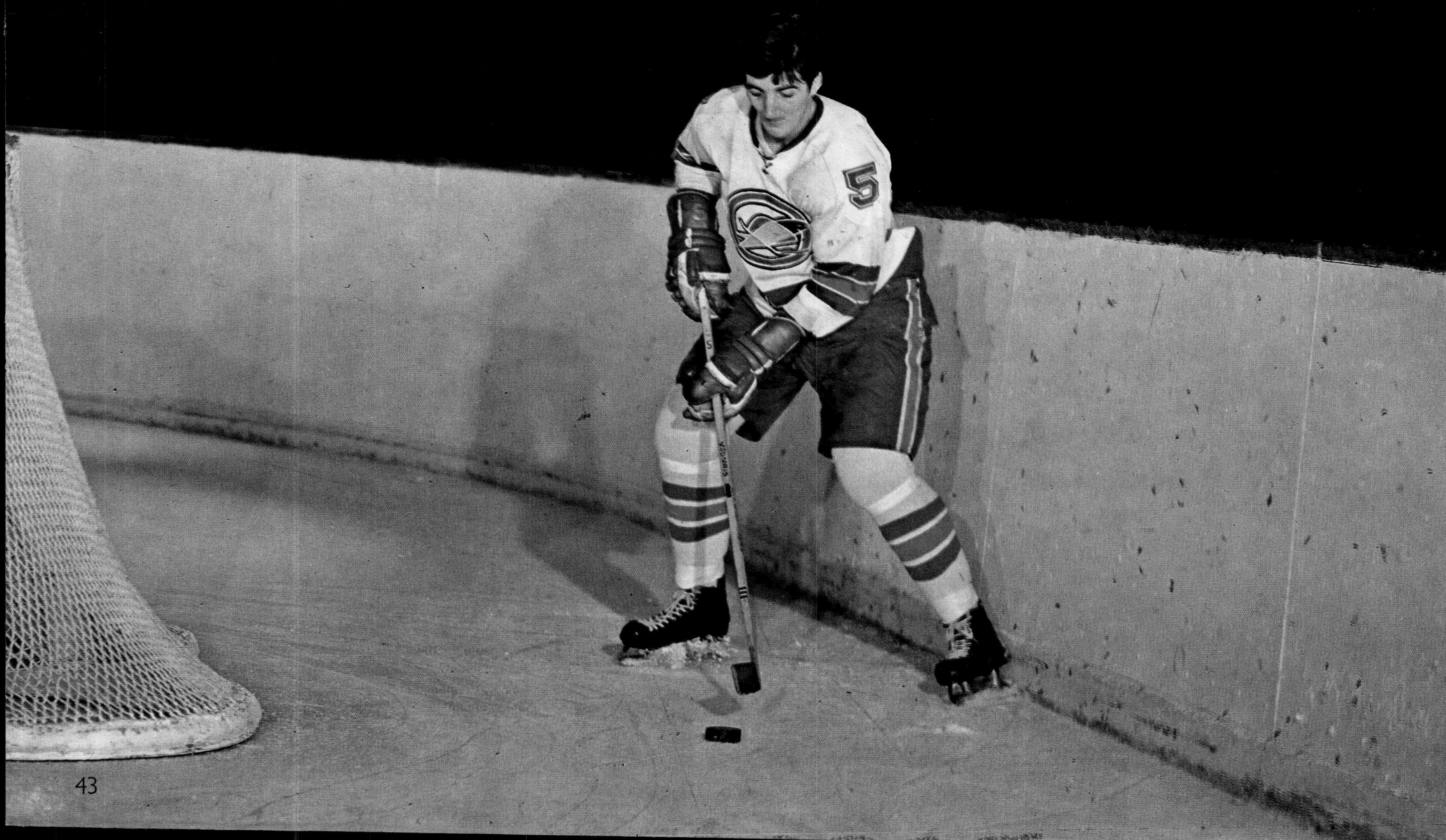

41

41 Bill White of the Los Angeles Kings,
who was twenty-eight before he had the
chance to play in the big league but
quickly proved himself to be one of the
steadiest defenders in the game.
42 Anticipation, strength, balance,
aggression—the defensive attributes
concentrated in this picture of Canadien
Ted Harris.
43 Harry Howell of the New York
Rangers demonstrates the perfect trip.
44 Doug Jarrett of the Black Hawks is
forced to use less conventional methods
to keep Ranger Hadfield out of the play.
Hadfield has something to say on the
subject.

45 Doug Harvey, one of the all-time great defenders, now assisting Scotty Bowman with the St Louis Blues, but still a power on the ice when required.
46 Former Leaf defenceman Allan Stanley is hard pressed to hold Montreal's Mr Hustle, the industrious Claude Provost.
47 Bobby Baun, in his Toronto days, demonstrates his defensive specialty, the solid body check.

48/49 The only two full-blooded Indians in the NHL. George Armstrong **48**, surrounded by Penguins and obviously discomfited, to the amusement of goalie Les Binkley. Jim Neilson **49**, one of the most improved defencemen in the league, but here having to deal with Eddie Shack and his imitation war-whoop.

50

51

50

50 Contrasting Canadien expressions in the goalmouth. Laperrière has the lean and hungry look; Gump Worsley his customary breathless demeanour.
51 Last line of defence. The Rangers get down on their knees to ward off the Pocket Rocket.
52 Jim Roberts of the St Louis Blues is one of the best all-round players in the league, but Toronto's Mike Walton has beaten him to it in this shot.

52

53

54

55

56

57

58

53/54/55 Gerry Desjardins of the Los Angeles Kings. This French-Canadian goalie is on the up and up, and was one of the most sought-after youngsters in hockey when Kings obtained him. **53** and **55** He saves from Toronto centre Murray Oliver. **54** Desjardins is on his knees, the puck in mid-air, and Bob Pulford ready to harass when it drops.

56/57/58 Doug Favell, the Philadelphia Flyers' young goalie. Since his first game as a professional, when he let in ten goals, Favell has never looked back. He is now not only one of the best goalies in the league, but also one of the most aggressive. **56** and **57** He saves twice acrobatically in a game with Toronto, but finally dives too late **58** to stop Ron Ellis's shot.

59/60/61/62/63 The veteran of them all, forty-four- (forty-five- ? forty-six- ?) year-old Johnny Bower. A master of his art and a supreme stylist, Bower is reckoned by doctors to have the physique and reflexes of a twenty-five year old.
59 Composure unruffled, he blocks a Chicago attack. **60**, **61**, **62**, **63** He demonstrates the importance of perfect positioning and co-ordination.

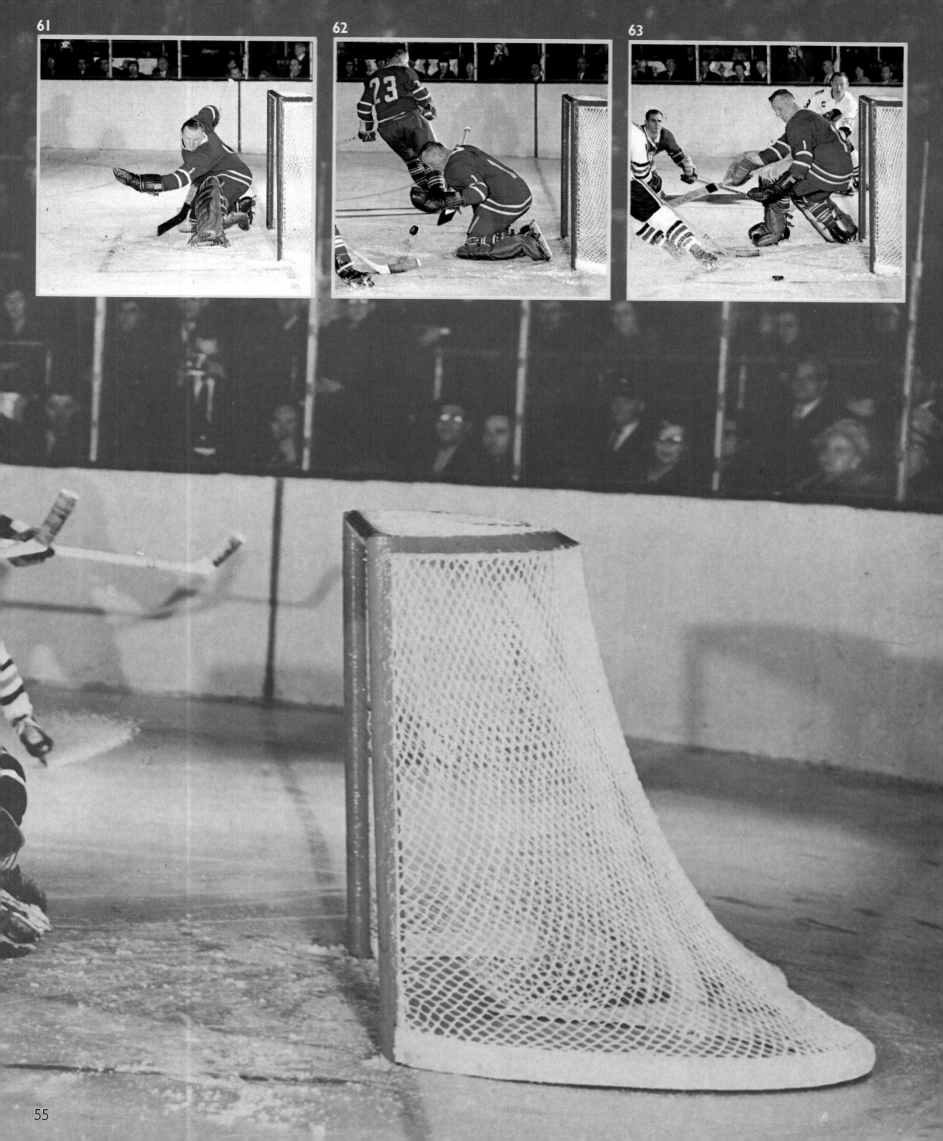

61

62

63

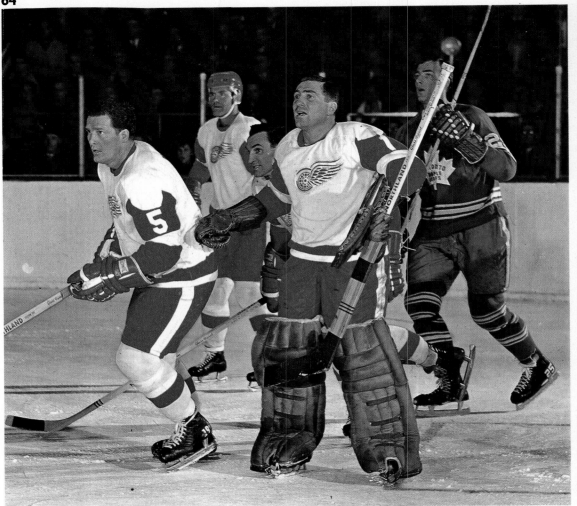

64/65/66 A goalie who makes up for his lack of stature with quick reflexes—Roger Crozier of the Red Wings. One of the few to make all-star in his rookie season, he has been bothered in recent seasons by the weaknesses in the Detroit defence. **64** His consternation is evident here, but **65** he appears to have this shot well covered. **66** Crozier stands no nonsense, though it is not clear with whom he has made contact.

66

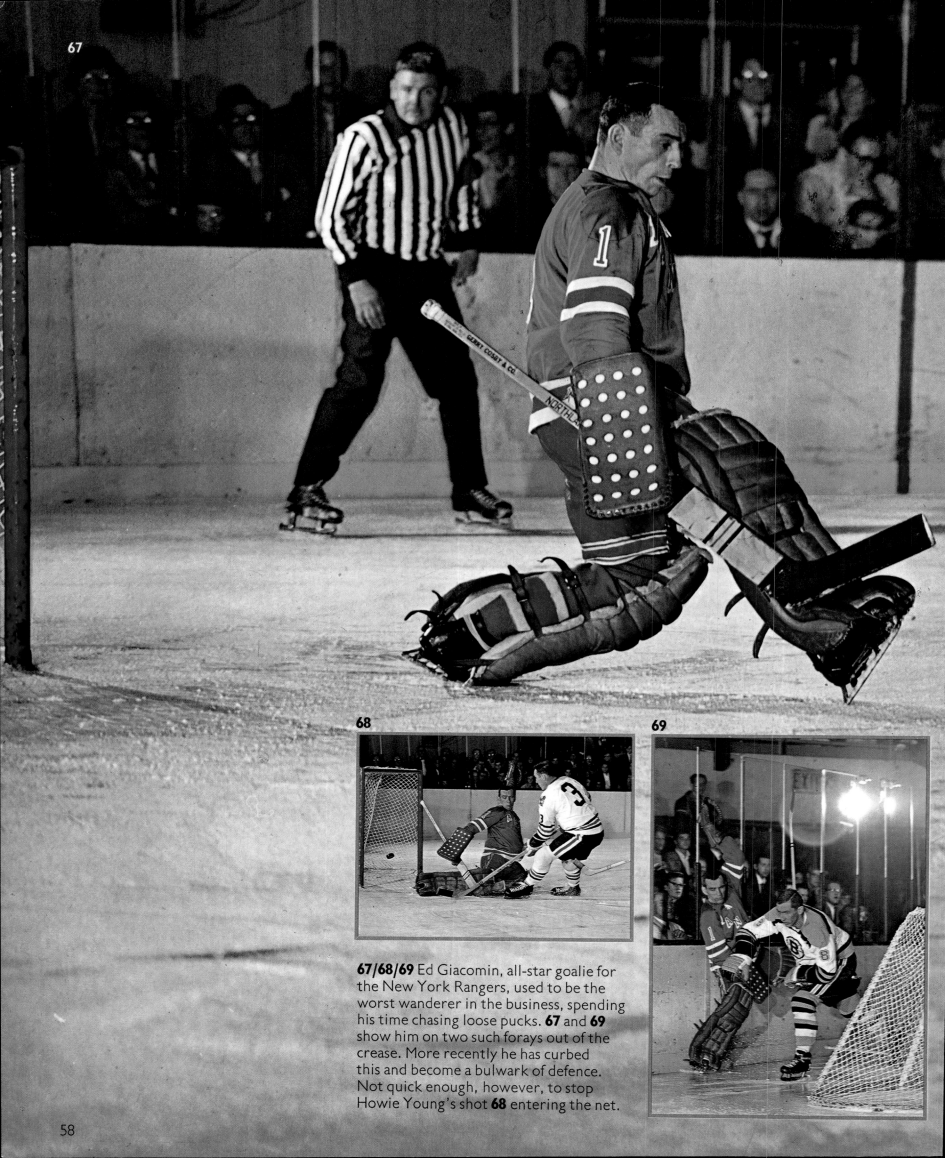

67

68

69

67/68/69 Ed Giacomin, all-star goalie for the New York Rangers, used to be the worst wanderer in the business, spending his time chasing loose pucks. **67** and **69** show him on two such forays out of the crease. More recently he has curbed this and become a bulwark of defence. Not quick enough, however, to stop Howie Young's shot **68** entering the net.

58

71

72

73

74

70/71/72/73/74 Lorne 'Gump' Worsley, Montreal Canadiens' outspoken, belligerent but invaluable goalie. Never noted for his style, he is remarkably agile and somehow manages to get that generous frame in front of most shots. **70** Here however Chico Maki of the Black Hawks has sent him the wrong way. **71**, **72**, **73**, **74** show the facial and physical contortions that have made him such a distinctive figure on the rink. More important to the Canadiens is that he makes saves, not faces. He does.

75

76

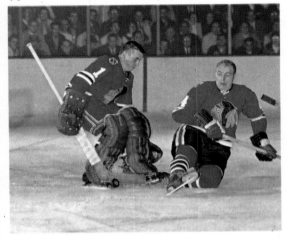

75/76 A surprise choice when the Boston Bruins acquired him, Gerry Cheevers has since more than justified their faith in him. **75** He looks younger than his twenty-eight years, but goalies can age quickly in this game. **76** Cheevers anxiously waits on the edge of his crease to deal with danger in the shape of the Big M.
77/78/79 Denis Dejordy of Chicago. The Black Hawks rate him high because he had to step into the gap left by the great Glenn Hall, and he did them proud. **77** and **78** Dejordy's cheerful demeanour on ice is a rare sight among goalies, most of whom, if they're not masked, are too bruised by their profession to manage it. **79** Dejordy goes down with Black Hawk defenceman Tom Reid to smother a shot.

80/81 Unmistakable. Jacques Plante in the Montreal goal in his hey-day. Famed for his innovations, Plante was the first man to wear a protective mask and the first goalie to leave his cage in pursuit of loose pucks. **80** Plante manages to stay in the crease to grab this one. **81** He watches a Black Hawk shot all the way into the glove.

82/83 Veteran Terry Sawchuk playing for and against the Detroit Red Wings with whom he had his most successful years. **82** Sawchuk saves for the Maple Leafs by taking it on his chest. **83** Here he has blocked Dave Keon's path but the puck is airborne.

84 Bruce Gamble who became Bower's full-time partner in the Maple Leaf goal when Sawchuk was transferred to Los Angeles in the expansion draft.
85 Les Binkley of the Penguins, who came into hockey as a trainer but is now highly respected between the posts. Some reckon that he has the fastest catching hand in the game.
86 Charlie Hodge, for years second-string goalie to Jacques Plante and Gump Worsley at Montreal, finally left in 1967 to join the Seals where he has brought solidity and experience to back up a young defence.

ROUGHING

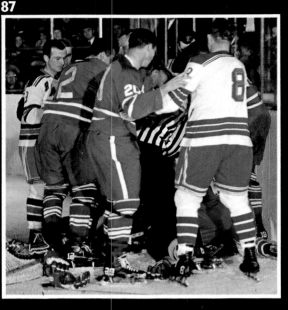

87/88 Rough house between the Rangers and the Maple Leafs. With so many gauntlets down, the scene resembles a medieval joust. Somebody is down **87**, but the participants quickly become dispirited or shamefaced **88**.

89/90/91/92 Fights on the ice can begin in any number of ways, but they usually end up with drawn blood and a major penalty. In this sequence Terry Harper of the Montreal Canadiens seems to be the offender, or the victim, as he squares up to a Maple Leaf **89**, is made to break by the referee **90**, and leaves the rink **91** with bloodstained face and shirt. The referee's task is certainly not an enviable one when he has to rush in **92** where angels would fear to tread.

89

90

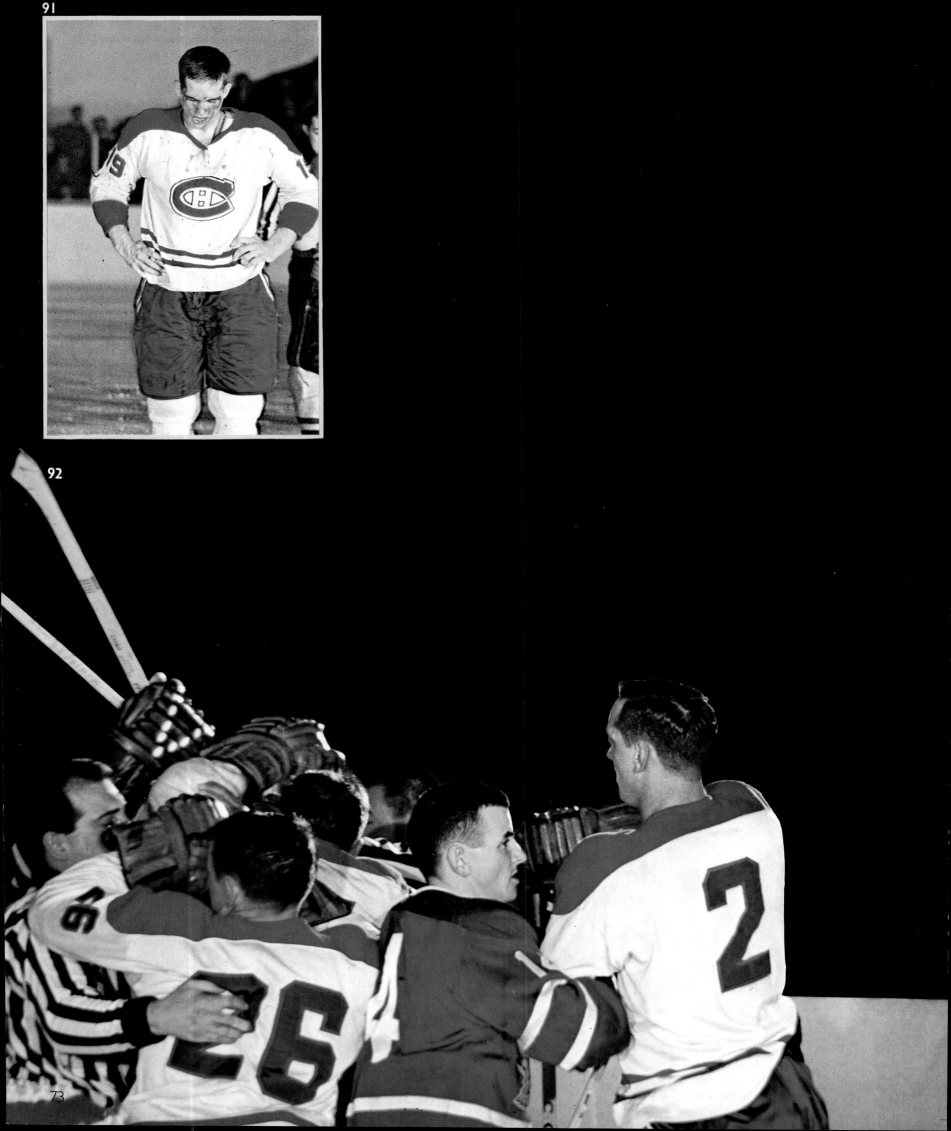

91

92

73

93

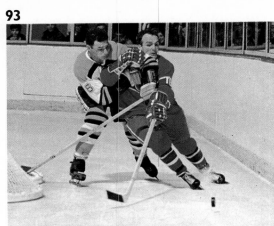

94

95  **96**  **97**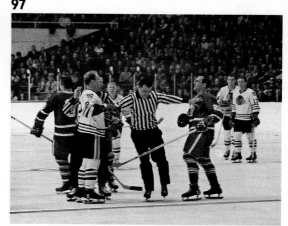

93/94 Ted Green of the Bruins has a reputation as a rough guy. **93** Here he is elbowing and pulling the Pocket Rocket in a race for the puck. **94** Green threatens to decapitate Eddie Shack (unlikely these days since they are teammates).

95/96/97 Bobby Baun adds punch to any team so the Red Wings, with their patchy defence, were glad to get him. Baun is known as a gourmet, but rarely personifies delicacy on the ice as in **95** where he is unceremoniously tripping and hooking Larry Mickey. **96** The clash of sticks as three tough guys converge—Baun, Yvan Cournoyer and John Ferguson. **97** Baun appears to have done enough to get Bobby Hull angry.

98 The bad boy who claims to have reformed—Howie Young. The fans may take some convincing though. So, too, the other players in the league.

99 A rare event. Red Kelly, former Member of Parliament, four times winner of the Lady Byng citation as the most gentlemanly player in hockey, a man who never raises his voice, got mad enough to lead with his right against Red Wing Gary Bergman.

100 They say that Bob Pulford has lost some of his aggressiveness but it seems that here he won't be content unless he can make off with at least one Red Wing's head.

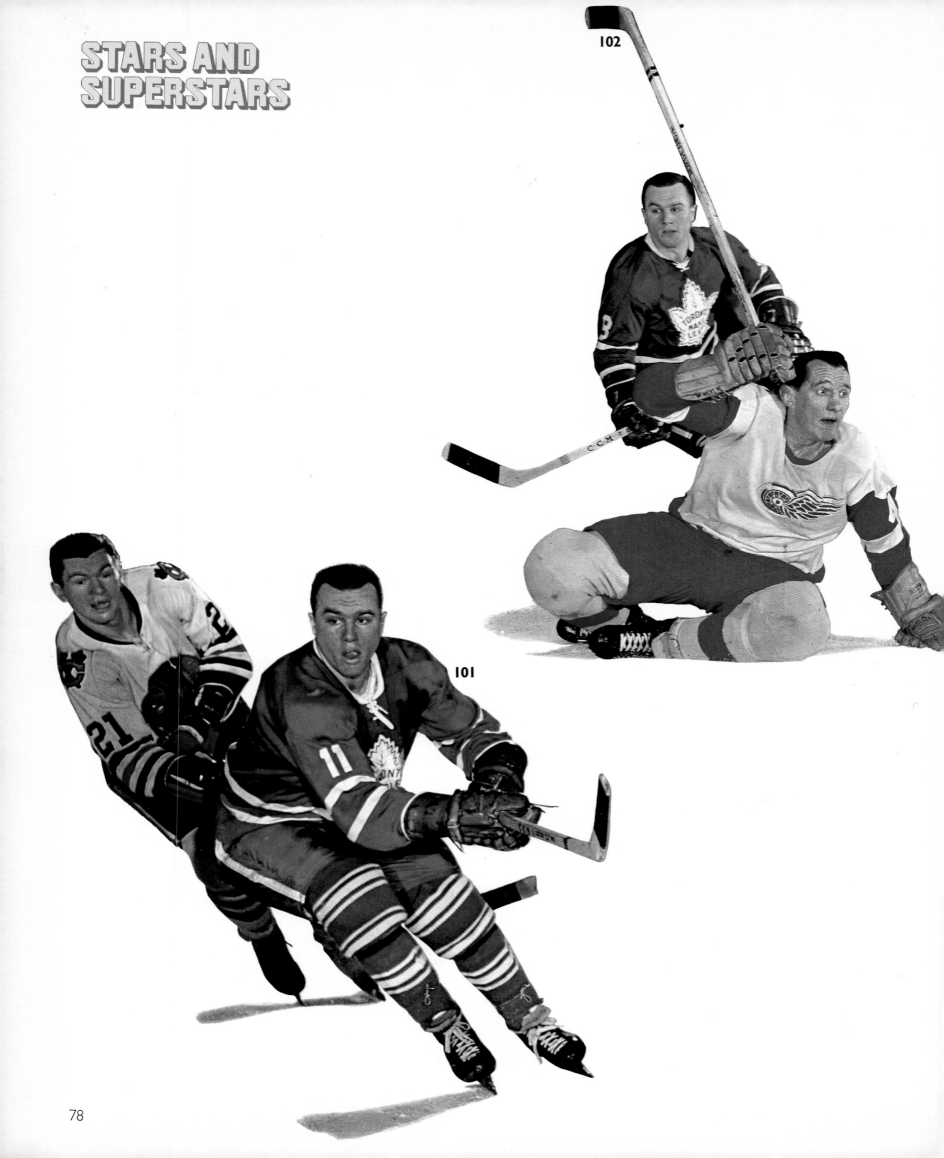

102

101

101/102 Ron Ellis in the company of two of the Greats. Ellis himself is only twenty-four and may well join the ranks of the superstars in the not too distant future. Leafs have certainly singled him out as being of exceptional promise. **101** Ellis has a fine turn of speed, more than necessary with Stan Mikita in pursuit. **102** The Great Gadsby is down but Ellis will know that he never gives up.

103/104/105/106 Three of the most prominent players in the NHL—Henri Richard, Jacques Laperrière and Rod Gilbert. Richard, no longer in his first youth and never the power that brother Maurice was in the game, has still plenty of menace left in him **103** (despite being tripped by Gilbert). **104** Laperrière is rooted but Gilbert is already on the move. Gilbert's elusive speed is one of the reasons why a really bright future is predicted for him. **105** Richard in a scoring position in front of the New York goal. **106** Laperrière, surrounded by all-stars, proves that height, a long reach and a big stride are invaluable assets.

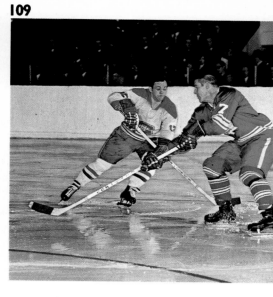

107/108 Bobby Rousseau is a vital link in the Montreal attack with his big shot and his gift for setting up goals. In 1966 he suffered a loss in confidence and the goals were hard to come by. Too intelligent a player to stay down for long, he rationalized his approach to the game, and is now back where he belongs—at the top and scoring goals.

109/110 One of the iron men in defence, Tim Horton has finally won recognition after long service in the league. He might have made all-star long ago if he had had iron in his soul as well as his body, but, as the Leafs claim, he is too nice a guy. **109** Horton is beaten by the speed of little Yvan Cournoyer, one of the most improved attackers in the game. **110** He looks mean anyway as he clashes with Rangers' Don Marshall.

110

111 Phil Esposito, who may take over Bobby Hull's mantle in the scoring records. Hull's partner for a time in the Black Hawk forward line, his value could not be properly assessed until he joined the Bruins and had to score goals on his own. Now the Bruins feel that they have a real winner in this powerful young player.

112 Frank Mahovlich, the Big M, has now come into his own with the Red Wings after years of frustration at Toronto. The Maple Leaf fans never really accepted him, and Mahovlich's easy disposition couldn't stand the pressure. It is not too late for him to blossom into the really big star he has always threatened to become.

113 Jean-Claude Tremblay, the Montreal quarter-back who stepped into the gap left by the great Doug Harvey, is a well-equipped all-round player. He has a powerful shot which the Canadiens have found more than useful on several occasions.

114 Rangers' captain Bob Nevin, whom the hockey purists believe to be one of the most complete forwards in the game, being superb in defence and lethal in attack. Certainly there are few who can understand why the Maple Leafs traded him in 1964.

115 Norm Ullman, here playing for the all-stars against teammate Marcel Pronovost. Ullman is one of the most self-effacing players in the league and one of the most efficient. With more than 300 goals to his credit, it was a surprise when Detroit decided to part with him.

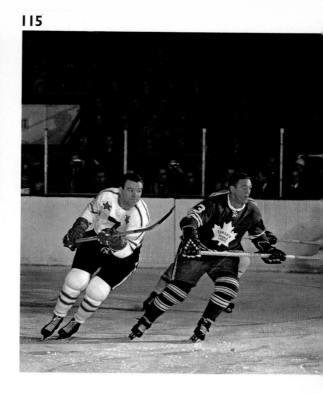

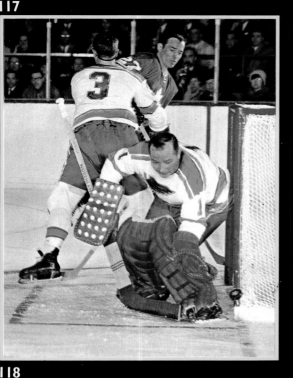

116 Bernie 'Boom-Boom' Geoffrion, who earned his nickname because of his explosive shot, is now coach to the Rangers. Geoffrion scored 393 goals during his playing career, a feat surpassed by only four others—Howe, the Rocket, Béliveau and Hull.

117/118 Glenn Hall, arguably the greatest goaltender hockey has known. Possessed of extraordinary eyesight and reflexes, Hall has created records all the way down the line. At one time in his career he played 552 consecutive matches, despite the fact that he suffers from bad nerves before each game. St Louis Blues were very happy to grab him as their first draft selection.

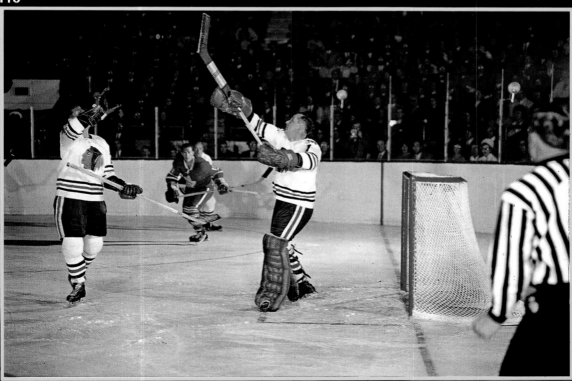

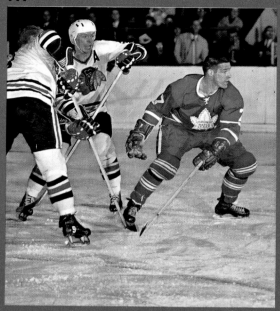

119/120/121 In his early years of big-time hockey Stan Mikita was a fighter with a chip on his shoulder. But suddenly he changed all that, won the Lady Byng Trophy, and developed into the complete player he is today. He is still approaching his prime so there is no limit to the scoring records he can amass and the devastation he can cause among opposing defences. The Hull-Mikita partnership in the Black Hawk forward line is of course Chicago's greatest asset. **119** Mikita helmeted and vociferous against the Maple Leafs; in a scoring position against the Rangers **120**. **121** No doubt about it, Mikita's curved stick, Gamble's contorted face and Toronto's bulging net tell the whole story.

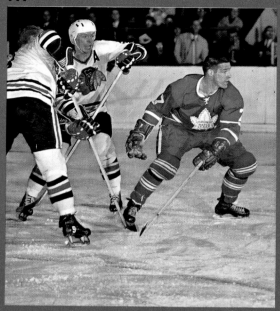

119

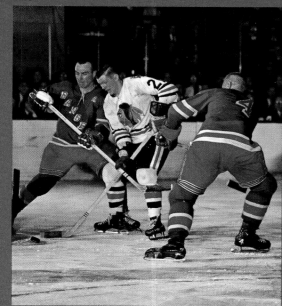

122/123/124 It seems superfluous to say anything about Bobby Hull because it has all been said before. The Golden Jet is certainly the biggest athlete the game has produced, and he is only thirty though it seems that he has been around for ever. His name is known all over the continent and he packs the crowds in wherever he goes. Only one thing may shorten his years in hockey—weariness. Forty-minute games are customary for him, and the pressure is on all the time as in **124** where the whole Montreal team are trying to stop him. **122**, **123** Hull's presence in front of goal means only one thing—trouble.

122

123

125/126/127 Every time he steps on to the ice he can't help breaking a record, and most of them are unlikely to be equalled. Certainly few will even come near to Gordie Howe's phenomenal total of goals, assists and all-star appearances. There is no sign of his powers waning either, in spite of a receding hairline and the opposition getting younger every year. His speed may have slipped a little, but he compensates for that by experience and anticipation, and reckons to join the defence when the pace of the forward line proves too hot. **125** Howe outwits Mahovlich and **126** Bower. **127** Classic pose of a great player.

125

126

128/129/130 Captain of the Canadiens, and chief folk hero of French Canada, Jean Béliveau's record is one of consistent dignity and class, both as a man and a player. Montreal are certainly worried about finding a replacement for him when he does retire because, when Béliveau has been injured, Canadiens have turned out to be pretty ordinary. Over his career he has averaged better than a point a game, which is one record he holds over Gordie Howe. In fact only Bobby Hull has matched it. **128** Playing for the all-stars he skates back into the attack with typical poise and grace. **129** Béliveau aggressive and **130** watchful.

128

129

131/132/133 A superstar of the future and a superstar of the past. Maurice Richard, the Rocket **131**, one of the greatest players ever produced by the Canadiens, who didn't once miss out on the all-star selections between 1943 and 1957. When he retired he had scored 544 goals. **132** and **133** Bobby Orr, Boston's star in the ascendant, who has such a brilliant array of talents that nobody can agree which is the greatest. After only two NHL seasons he won the Norris Memorial Trophy and joined the ranks of the all-stars. There is only one cloud on the horizon—Orr's knees persist in giving him trouble.

131

132

133